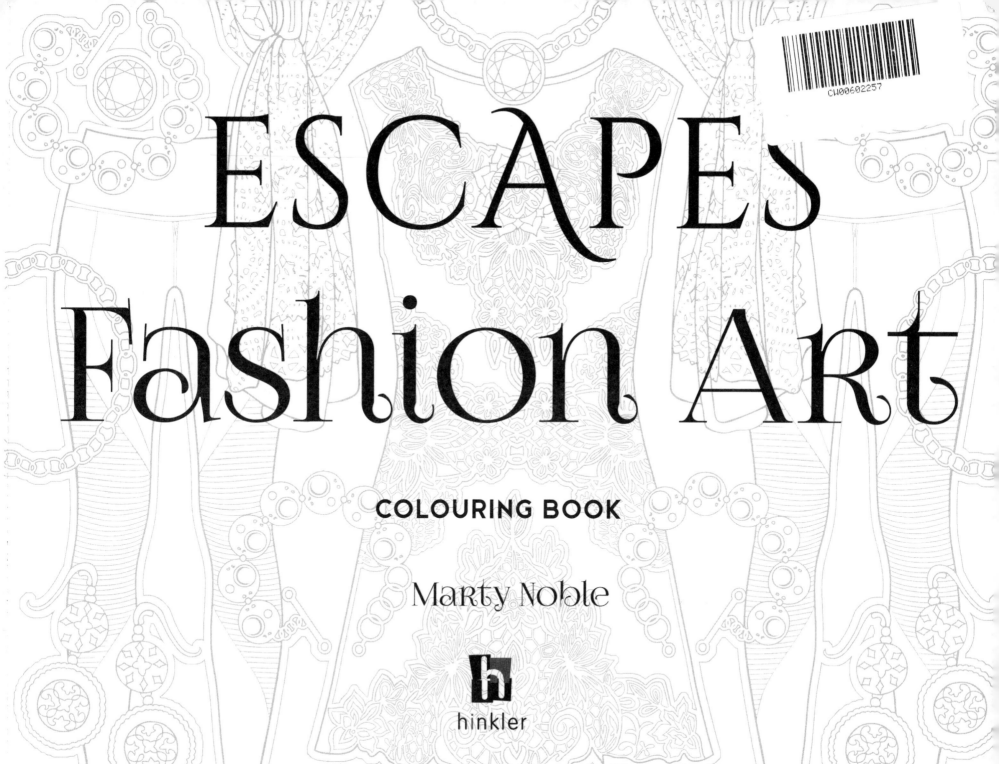

ESCAPES
Fashion Art

COLOURING BOOK

Marty Noble

hinkler

This beautifully detailed colouring book will appeal to budding artists and experienced colourists alike – especially those who enjoy fashion! There are over 50 drawings in this collection, which features unique collages of stunning clothing designs and accessories from vintage to modern fashion, as well as models portraying these styles. Acting as perfect canvasses for experimentation with media and colour techniques, these one-sided pages are perforated so that you can easily remove, colour and display your own runway fashion style!

ESCAPES Collage Art Coloring Book was first published by Dover
Publications, Inc., in 2016

This edition of *ESCAPES Collage Art Coloring Book* is published
by Hinkler Books Pty Ltd 2017

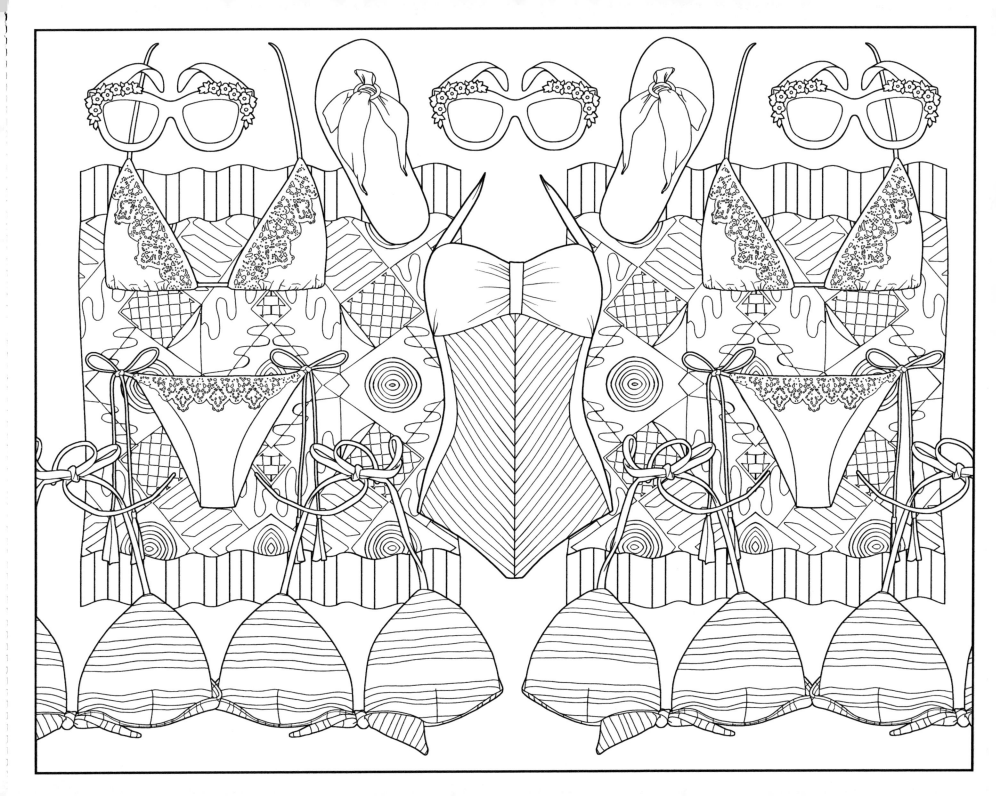

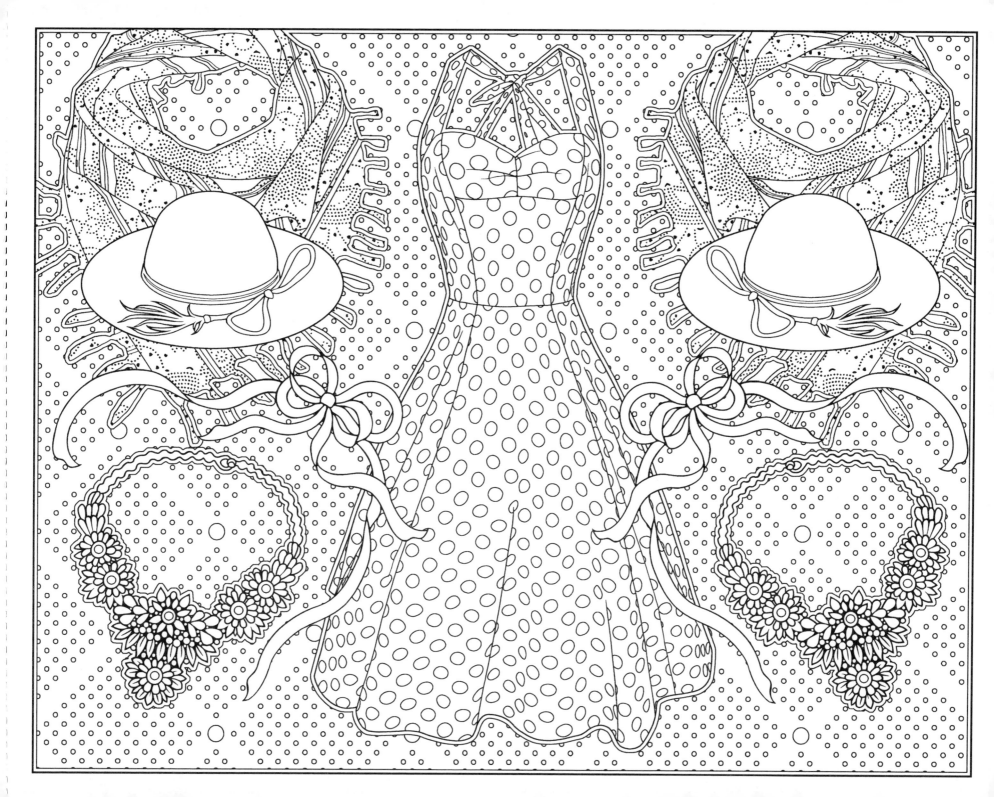

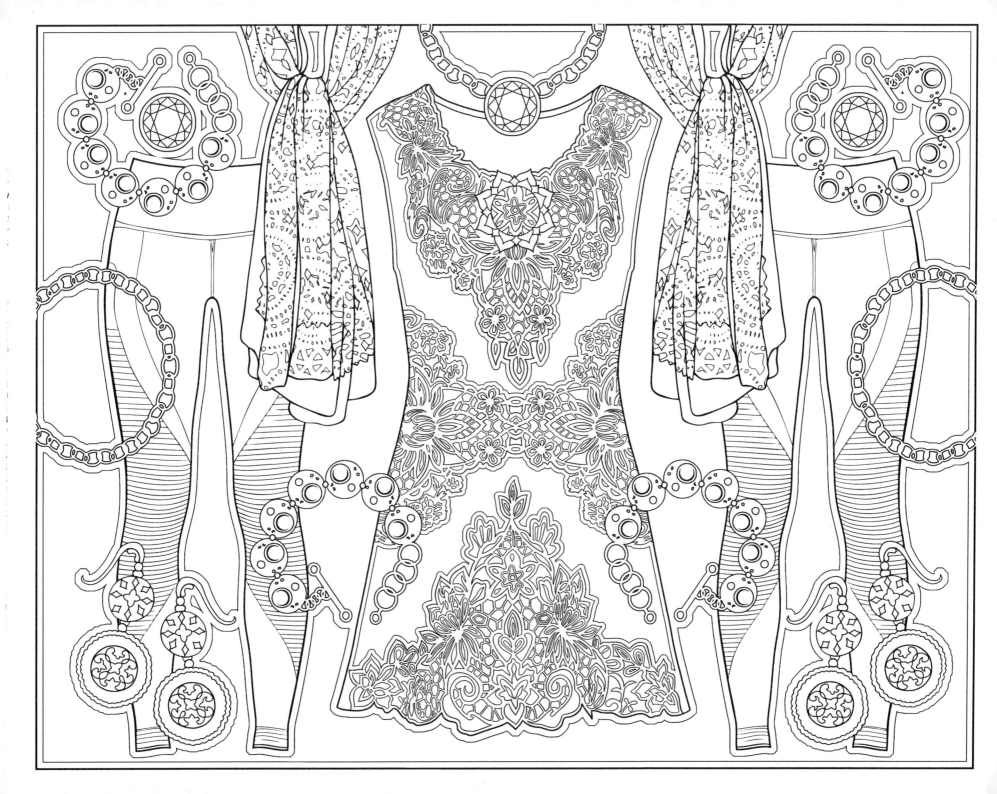